Oscar W

Quotes & Facts

By Blago Kirov

First Edition

*****

Oscar Wilde: Quotes & Facts
*****

Foreword

"I have nothing to declare except my genius."

This book is an anthology of 230 brilliant quotes and aphorisms from Oscar Wilde and selected facts about Oscar Wilde. It grants his reflections on subjects ranging from Genius to Stupidity; in addition, the book shows the personality of Oscar Wilde into a different, more human light:

Oscar Wilde's mother wanted a girl and often dressed the young Oscar in girls' clothing.
Oscar Wilde's Dorian Gray was based on John Gray, an incredibly handsome blond poet that Wilde met in 1889.
Oscar Wilde's mother was a feminist.
Oscar Wilde died bankrupt, and his friends could only afford a sixth-class burial.
Wilde married Constance Lloyd, daughter of wealthy Queen's Counsel Horace Lloyd, on May 29, 1884 and had two sons, Cyril and Vyvyan.
Wilde's intimate association with Alfred Douglas led to his trial on charges of homosexuality, then illegal in Britain. He was sentenced two years hard labor for the crime of sodomy.
Oscar Wilde changed his name by the time of his death to Sebastian Melmoth. He called himself Sebastien because he loved a portrait of St Sebastien and Melmoth after the book "Melmoth the Wanderer", which was written by his mother's uncle.
Oscar Wilde's father had three illegitimate children before he married Jane Francesca Elegee.

"I have nothing to declare except my genius."
"The only way to get rid of temptation is to yield to it."

"I love to talk about nothing. It's the only thing I know anything about."

"There is no sin except stupidity."

"Some things are too important to be taken seriously."

"Art is the only serious thing in the world. And the artist is the only person who is never serious."

"Women are meant to be loved, not to be understood."

"Every woman is a rebel."

"Everything popular is wrong."

"Only dull people are brilliant at breakfast."

"The world is a stage and the play is badly cast."

"Paradoxically though it may seem, it is none the less true that life imitates art far more than art imitates life."

Some Facts about Oscar Wilde

Oscar Wilde's mother wanted a girl and often dressed the young Oscar in girls' clothing.

Oscar Wilde's Dorian Gray was based on John Gray, an incredibly handsome blond poet that Wilde met in 1889.

Oscar Wilde's mother was a feminist.

Oscar Wilde died bankrupt, and his friends could only afford a sixth-class burial.

Wilde married Constance Lloyd, daughter of wealthy Queen's Counsel Horace Lloyd, on May 29, 1884 and had two sons, Cyril and Vyvyan.

Wilde's intimate association with Alfred Douglas led to his trial on charges of homosexuality, then illegal in Britain. He was sentenced two years hard labor for the crime of sodomy.

Oscar Wilde changed his name by the time of his death to Sebastian Melmoth. He called himself Sebastien because he loved a portrait of St Sebastien and Melmoth after the book "Melmoth the Wanderer", which was written by his mother's uncle.

Oscar Wilde's father had three illegitimate children before he married Jane Francesca Elegee.

Wilde's full name is "Oscar Fingal O'Flahertie Wills Wilde", born in Dublin in 1854.

Wilde's mother, Jane Wilde was a successful poet and Irish nationalist whose pen name was "Sperenza."

Wilde's father was well known Queen Victoria's eye surgeon and was knighted for it.

Wilde embarked on a tour of America in 1882 and held talks on a wide variety of subjects from "The English Renaissance" to "Decorative Art."

Wilde's son Cyril fought and died in World War I in the Battle of Festubert in France where he is buried.

His son Vyvyav changed his last name to Holland, like his mother, after his father's imprisonment and went on to become a translator for the BBC and author of the autobiography "Son of Oscar Wilde" (1954).

Wilde's grandson, Merlin Holland, published the Oscar Wilde biography "A Portrait of Oscar Wilde"

Oscar Wilde only published one novel, "The Portait of Dorian Gray"(1891).

Oscar Wilde's father was once accused of raping his patient while she was under anesthesia.

Oscar Wilde was an advocate of socialism and in his only political essay "The Soul of Man under Socialism" (1891) he expounds an anarchist philosophy.

Before his death due to cerebral meningitis Oscar Wilde was conditionally baptized in the Catholic Church.

Oscar Wilde's last words were "My wallpaper and I are fighting a duel to the death. One or other of us has got to go."

Oscar Wilde's tomb was designed by Sir Jacob Epstein.

Oscar Wilde wrote and produced nine plays.

Oscar Wilde published his collected Poems in 1881, when he was twenty-seven years old.

When Wilde went through U.S. customs in 1882, he said, "I have nothing to declare except my genius."

After Oscar Wilde's younger sister, Isola Emily Francesca, died at the age of ten, Wilde carried a lock of her hair with him for the rest of his life.

Oscar Wilde was a contemporary and acquaintance of the French symbolist poet, Stephane Mallarme.

At age 23, Oscar Wilde almost married Florence Blacombe, who instead married another famous writer, Bram Stoker, the author of Dracula.

Nine biographies have been written on Wilde since his death.

Oscar Wilde's dramatic tragedy, "Salome," was written in French and was performed in both Paris and London.

When Oscar Wilde met Jefferson Davis, the Confederate president, Wilde said that the South and Ireland had similar backgrounds.

Oscar Wilde was born in Dublin.

Oscar Wilde was awarded a scholarship to Trinity College Dublin.

From Trinity College Dublin Oscar Wilde won a scholarship to Magdalen College Oxford University.

While at Magdalen College, Wilde began wearing his hair long and openly scorning so-called "manly" sports, and began decorating his rooms with peacock feathers, lilies, sunflowers, blue china and other objects d'art.

Wilde's sexual orientation was bisexual and homosexual: he may have had significant sexual relationships with Frank Miles, Constance Lloyd (his wife), Robert Baldwin Ross, and Lord Alfred Douglas ("Bosie"). Wilde also had numerous sexual encounters with working-class male youths, who were often rent boys.

On his release from prison Oscar Wilde left for Paris where he lived in comparative anonymity.

'De Profundis' was written while in prison and recounts his thoughts and feelings on his incarceration.

Oscar Wilde died of cerebral meningitis on 30th November 1900 in Paris.

Oscar Wilde is buried at Pere Lachaise Cemetery, Paris.

Despite Wilde's preference for men and the social scandal caused by his trial and imprisonment, Wilde and his wife never divorced.

His Words

"I have nothing to declare except my genius."

"The only way to get rid of temptation is to yield to it."

"I love to talk about nothing. It's the only thing I know anything about."

"There is no sin except stupidity."

"Some things are too important to be taken seriously."

"Art is the only serious thing in the world. And the artist is the only person who is never serious."

"Women are meant to be loved, not to be understood."

"Every woman is a rebel."

"Everything popular is wrong."

"Only dull people are brilliant at breakfast."

"The world is a stage and the play is badly cast."

"Paradoxically though it may seem, it is none the less true that life imitates art far more than art imitates life."

"A bore is someone who deprives you of solitude without providing you with company."

"A cynic is a man who knows the price of everything, and the value of nothing."

"A gentleman is one who never hurts anyone's feelings unintentionally."

"A good friend will always stab you in the front."

"A kiss may ruin a human life"

"A little sincerity is a dangerous thing, and a great deal of it is absolutely fatal."

"A man can be happy with any woman as long as he does not love her."

"A man who does not think for himself does not think at all."

"A man's face is his autobiography. A woman's face is her work of fiction."

"A passion for pleasure is the secret of remaining young."

"A pessimist is somebody who complains about the noise when opportunity knocks."

"A thing is not necessarily true because a man dies for it."

"After a good dinner one can forgive anybody, even one's own relations."

"After the first glass, you see things as you wish they were. After the second, you see things as they are not. Finally, you see things as they really are, and that is the most horrible thing in the world."

"Ah! The strength of women comes from the fact that psychology cannot explain us. Men can be analyzed, women...merely adored."

"All art is quite useless."

"All women become like their mothers. That is their tragedy. No man does, and that is his."

"Always forgive your enemies; nothing annoys them so much."

"Always! That is a dreadful word. It makes me shudder when I hear it. Women are so fond of using it. They spoil every romance by trying to make it last forever. It is a meaningless word, too. The only difference between a caprice and a life-long passion is that the caprice lasts a little longer."

"America has never quite forgiven Europe for having been discovered somewhat earlier in history than itself."

"America is the only country that went from barbarism to decadence without civilization in between."

"An idea that is not dangerous is unworthy of being called an idea at all."

"Anybody can sympathize with the sufferings of a friend, but it requires a very fine nature to sympathise with a friend's success."

"Anyone who lives within their means suffers from a lack of imagination."

"As long as a woman can look ten years younger than her daughter, she is perfectly satisfied"

"Be yourself; everyone else is already taken."

"Behind every exquisite thing that existed, there was something tragic."

"Between men and women there is no friendship possible. There is passion, enmity, worship, love, but no friendship."

"Bigamy is having one wife too many. Monogamy is the same."

"Children begin by loving their parents; as they grow older they judge them; sometimes they forgive them."

"Conformity is the last refuge of the unimaginative."

"Consistency is the hallmark of the unimaginative."

"Crying is for plain women. Pretty women go shopping."

"Death must be so beautiful: to lie in the soft brown earth, with the grasses waving above one's head, and listen to silence; to have no yesterday, and no tomorrow;to forget time, to forgive life, to be at peace."

"Deceiving others. That is what the world calls a romance."

"Disobedience, in the eyes of any one who has read history, is human's original virtue. It is through disobedience that progress has been made, through disobedience and through rebellion."

"Each of us has heaven and hell in him..."

"Education is an admirable thing, but it is well to remember from time to time that nothing that is worth knowing can be taught."

"Every portrait that is painted with feeling is a portrait of the artist, not of the sitter."

"Every saint has a past, and every sinner has a future."

"Everything in the world is about sex except sex. Sex is about power."

"Experience is merely the name men gave to their mistakes."

"Experience is one thing you can't get for nothing."

"Fashion is a form of ugliness so intolerable that we have to alter it every six months."

"For one moment our lives met, our souls touched."

"Friendship is far more tragic than love. It lasts longer."

"He has no enemies, but is intensely disliked by his friends."

"Hear no evil, speak no evil, and you won't be invited to cocktail parties."

"Hearts Live By Being Wounded"

"How can a woman be expected to be happy with a man who insists on treating her as if she were a perfectly normal human being"

"How you can sit there, calmly eating muffins when we are in this horrible trouble, I can't make out. You seem to me to be perfectly heartless."

"Humanity takes itself too seriously. It is the world's original sin. If the cave-man had known how to laugh, History would have been different."

"I adore simple pleasures. They are the last refuge of the complex."

"I am not young enough to know everything."

"I am sick of women who love one. Women who hate one are much more interesting."

"I am so clever that sometimes I don't understand a single word of what I am saying."

"I am tired of myself to-night. I should like to be somebody else."

"I am too fond of reading books to care to write them."

"I can resist anything except temptation."

"I choose my friends for their good looks, my acquaintances for their good characters, and my enemies for their good intellects."

"I don't say we all ought to misbehave. But we ought to look as if we could"

"I don't like compliments, and I don't see why a man should think he is pleasing a woman enormously when he says to her a whole heap of things that he doesn't mean."

"I don't want to be at the mercy of my emotions. I want to use them, to enjoy them, and to dominate them."

"I don't want to go to heaven. None of my friends are there."

"I hate people who are not serious about meals. It is so shallow of them."

"I have grown to love secrecy. It seems to be the one thing that can make modern life mysterious or marvelous to us. The commonest thing is delightful if only one hides it."

"I have learned this: it is not what one does that is wrong, but what one becomes as a consequence of it."

"I have no objection to anyone's sex life as long as they don't practice it in the street and frighten the horses."

"I have the simplest tastes. I am always satisfied with the best."

"I hope you have not been leading a double life, pretending to be wicked and being good all the time. That would be hypocrisy."

"I knew nothing but shadows and I thought them to be real."

"I like men who have a future and women who have a past."

"I like persons better than principles, and I like persons with no principles better than anything else in the world."

"I love acting. It is so much more real than life."

"I may not agree with you, but I will defend to the death your right to make an ass of yourself."

"I never change, except in my affections."

"I never put off till tomorrow what I can possibly do - the day after."

"I never travel without my diary. One should always have something sensational to read in the train."

"I really don't see anything romantic in proposing. It is very romantic to be in love. But there is nothing romantic about a definite proposal. Why, one may be accepted. One usually is, I believe. Then the excitement is all over. The very essence of romance is uncertainty. If ever I get married, I'll certainly try to forget the fact."

"I see when men love women. They give them but a little of their lives. But women when they love give everything."

"I think God, in creating man, somewhat overestimated his ability."

"I was working on the proof of one of my poems all the morning, and took out a comma. In the afternoon I put it back again."

"I wonder who it was defined man as a rational animal. It was the most premature definition ever given. Man is many things, but he is not rational."

"I won't tell you that the world matters nothing, or the world's voice, or the voice of society. They matter a good deal. They matter far too much. But there are moments when one has to choose between living one's own life, fully, entirely, completely — or dragging out some false, shallow, degrading existence that the world in its hypocrisy demands. You have that moment now. Choose!"

"If I am occasionally a little over-dressed, I make up for it by being always immensely over-educated."

"If one cannot enjoy reading a book over and over again, there is no use in reading it at all."

"If you are not long, I will wait for you all my life."

"If you want to be a doormat you have to lay yourself down first."

"If you want to tell people the truth, make them laugh, otherwise they'll kill you."

"I'll bet you anything you like that half an hour after they have met, they will be calling each other sister.

"Illusion is the first of all pleasures"

"In matters of grave importance, style, not sincerity, is the vital thing."

"In old days books were written by men of letters and read by the public. Nowadays books are written by the public and read by nobody."

"In this world there are only two tragedies. One is not getting what one wants, and the other is getting it. (Mr. Dumby, Act III)"

"Indeed I have always been of the opinion that hard work is simply the refuge of people who have nothing to do."

"Irony is wasted on the stupid"

"It is absurd to divide people into good and bad. People are either charming or tedious."

"It is only shallow people who do not judge by appearances. The true mystery of the world is the visible, not the invisible...."

"It is the stupid and the ugly who have the best of it in this world"

"It is what you read when you don't have to that determines what you will be when you can't help it."

"It takes great courage to see the world in all its tainted glory, and still to love it. And even more courage to see it in the one you love"

"Keep love in your heart. A life without it is like a sunless garden when the flowers are dead. The consciousness of loving and being loved brings a warmth and a richness to life that nothing else can bring."

"Laughter is not at all a bad beginning for a friendship, and it is by far the best ending for one."

"Life has been your art. You have set yourself to music. Your days are your sonnets."

"Life is far too important a thing ever to talk seriously about."

"Life is never fair, and perhaps it is a good thing for most of us that it is not."

"Life is not complex. We are complex. Life is simple, and the simple thing is the right thing."

"Life is too short to learn German"

"Live! Live the wonderful life that is in you! Let nothing be lost upon you. Be always searching for new sensations. Be afraid of nothing."

"Man is least himself when he talks in his own person. Give him a mask, and he will tell you the truth."

"Memory is the diary we all carry about with us."

"Men always want to be a woman's first love. That is their clumsy vanity. We women have a more subtle instinct about these things. What (women) like is to be a man's last romance."

"Men marry because they are tired; women, because they are curious: both are disappointed."

"Misfortunes one can endure--they come from outside, they are accidents. But to suffer for one's own faults-- ah!--there is the sting of life."

"Moderation is a fatal thing. Nothing succeeds like excess."

"Morality is simply the attitude we adopt towards people we personally dislike."

"Most people are other people. Their thoughts are someone else's opinions, their lives a mimicry, their passions a quotation."

"Music makes one feel so romantic - at least it always gets on one's nerves - which is the same thing nowadays."

"My own business always bores me to death; I prefer other people's."

"Never love anyone who treats you like you're ordinary."

"Never marry at all, Dorian. Men marry because they are tired, women, because they are curious: both are disappointed."

"Never speak disrespectfully of Society, Algernon. Only people who can't get into it do that."

"No good deed goes unpunished."

"No man is rich enough to buy back his past."

"Nothing can cure the soul but the senses, just as nothing can cure the senses but the soul."

"Nothing that is worth knowing can be taught"

"Nowadays most people die of a sort of creeping common sense, and discover when it is too late that the only things one never regrets are one's mistakes."

"Nowadays people know the price of everything and the value of nothing."

"Oh, brothers! I don't care for brothers. My elder brother won't die, and my younger brothers seem never to do anything else."

"One can always be kind to people about whom one cares nothing."

"One has a right to judge a man by the effect he has over his friends."

"One should always be a little improbable."

"One should always be in love. That's the reason one should never marry."

"One should always play fairly when one has the winning cards."

"One should never trust a woman who tells one her real age. A woman who would tell one that would tell one anything."

"One's real life is so often the life that one does not lead."

"Only the shallow know themselves"

"Ordinary riches can be stolen, real riches cannot. In your soul are infinitely precious things that cannot be taken from you."

"People who count their chickens before they are hatched act very wisely because chickens run about so absurdly that it's impossible to count them accurately."

"Popularity is the one insult I have never suffered."

"Punctuality is the thief of time"

"Quotation is a serviceable substitute for wit."

"Selfishness is not living as one wishes to live, it is asking others to live as one wishes to live."

"She behaves as if she was beautiful. Most American women do. It is the secret of their charm."

"She is all the great heroines of the world in one. She is more than an individual. I love her, and I must make her love me. I want to make Romeo jealous. I want the dead lovers of the world to hear our laughter, and grow sad. I want a breath of our passion to stir dust into consciousness, to wake their ashes into pain. "

"She is very clever, too clever for a woman. She lacks the indefinable charm of weakness."

"She...can talk brilliantly upon any subject provided she knows nothing about it."

"Sin is a thing that writes itself across a man's face. It cannot be concealed."

"Society often forgives the criminal; it never forgives the dreamer."

"Some cause happiness wherever they go; others whenever they go."

"Some things are more precious because they don't last long."

"The basis of optimism is sheer terror."

"The books that the world calls immoral are books that show the world its own shame."

"The difference between literature and journalism is that journalism is unreadable and literature is not read."

"The good ended happily, and the bad unhappily. That is what Fiction means."

"The heart was made to be broken."

"The most terrible thing about it is not that it breaks one's heart — hearts are made to be broken — but that it turns one's heart to stone."

"The mystery of love is greater than the mystery of death."

"The nicest feeling in the world is to do a good deed anonymously-and have somebody find out."

"The one charm of the past is that it is the past."

"The only artists I have ever known who are personally delightful are bad artists. Good artists exist simply in what they make, and consequently are perfectly uninteresting in what they are. A great poet, a really great poet, is the most unpoetical of all creatures. But inferior poets are absolutely fascinating. The worse their rhymes are, the more picturesque they look. The mere fact of having published a book of second-rate sonnets makes a man quite irresistible. He lives the poetry that he cannot write. The others write the poetry that they dare not realize."

"The only good thing to do with good advice is pass it on; it is never of any use to oneself."

"The only way a woman can ever reform a man is by boring him so completely that he loses all possible interest in life."

"The public have an insatiable curiosity to know everything, except what is worth knowing."

"The public is wonderfully tolerant. It forgives everything except genius."

"The reason we all like to think so well of others is that we are all afraid for ourselves. The basis of optimism is sheer terror."

"The suspense is terrible. I hope it will last."

"The truth is rarely pure and never simple."

"The very essence of romance is uncertainty."

"The world is changed because you are made of ivory and gold. The curves of your lips rewrite history."

"The world was my oyster but I used the wrong fork."

"There are many things that we would throw away if we were not afraid that others might pick them up."

"There are moments when one has to choose between living one's own life, fully, entirely, completely-or dragging out some false, shallow, degrading existence that the world in its hypocrisy demands."

"There are only two kinds of people who are really fascinating: people who know absolutely everything, and people who know absolutely nothing."

"There is a luxury in self-reproach. When we blame ourselves, we feel that no one else has a right to blame us. It is the confession, not the priest, that gives us absolution."

"There is no such thing as a moral or an immoral book. Books are well written, or badly written. That is all."

"There is only one class in the community that thinks more about money than the rich, and that is the poor."

"There is only one thing in the world worse than being talked about, and that is not being talked about."

"There was so much in you that charmed me that I felt I must tell you something about yourself. I thought how tragic it would be if you were wasted."

"They get up early, because they have so much to do, and go to bed early, because they have so little to think about. "

"They've promised that dreams can come true - but forgot to mention that nightmares are dreams, too."

"Those who are faithful know only the trivial side of love: it is the faithless who know love's tragedies."

"Those who find ugly meanings in beautiful things are corrupt without being charming. This is a fault. Those who find beautiful meanings in beautiful things are the cultivated. For these there is hope. They are the elect to whom beautiful things mean only Beauty. There is no such thing as a moral or an immoral book. Books are well written, or badly written. That is all."

"To be popular one must be a mediocrity."

"To define is to limit."

"To get back my youth I would do anything in the world, except take exercise, get up early, or be respectable."

"To live is the rarest thing in the world. Most people exist, that is all."

"To lose one parent may be regarded as a misfortune; to lose both looks like carelessness."

"To love oneself is the beginning of a lifelong romance."

"Ultimately the bond of all companionship, whether in marriage or in friendship, is conversation, and conversation must have a common basis, and between two people of widely different culture the only common basis possible is the lowest level."

"We are all in the gutter, but some of us are looking at the stars."

"We are each our own devil, and we make this world our hell."

"We live in an age when unnecessary things are our only necessities."

"We women, as some one says, love with our ears, just as you men love with your eyes..."

"What does it profit a man if he gain the whole world and lose his own soul?"

"When a woman marries again, it is because she detested her first husband. When a man marries again, it is because he adored his first wife. Women try their luck; men risk theirs."

"When one is in love, one always begins by deceiving one's self, and one always ends by deceiving others. That is what the world calls a romance."

"When the Gods wish to punish us, they answer our prayers."

"Whenever a man does a thoroughly stupid thing, it is always from the noblest motives."

"Whenever people agree with me I always feel I must be wrong."

"Where there is sorrow, there is holy ground."

"Who, being loved, is poor?"

"Wickedness is a myth invented by good people to account for the curious attractiveness of others."

"With freedom, books, flowers, and the moon, who could not be happy?"

"Women have a much better time than men in this world; there are far more things forbidden to them."

"Words! Mere words! How terrible they were! How clear, and vivid, and cruel! One could not escape from them. And yet what a subtle magic there was in them! They seemed to be able to give a plastic form to formless things, and to have a music of their own as sweet as that of viol or of lute. Mere words! Was there anything so real as words?"

"Work is the curse of the drinking classes."

"Yes: I am a dreamer. For a dreamer is one who can only find his way by moonlight, and his punishment is that he sees the dawn before the rest of the world."

"You can never be overdressed or overeducated."

"You don't love someone for their looks, or their clothes, or for their fancy car, but because they sing a song only you can hear."

"You like every one; that is to say, you are indifferent to every one."

"You must have a cigarette. A cigarette is the perfect type of a perfect pleasure. It is exquisite, and it leaves one unsatisfied. What more can one want?"

"You will always be fond of me. I represent to you all the sins you never had the courage to commit."

"Youth is wasted on the young."

Printed in Great Britain
by Amazon